EROSION

By Anna McDougal

Please visit our website, www.enslow.com. For a free color catalog of all our high-quality books, call toll free 1-800-398-2504 or fax 1-877-980-4454.

Cataloging-in-Publication Data

Names: McDougal, Anna.
Title: Erosion / Anna McDougal.
Description: New York : Enslow Publishing, 2024. | Series: Earth's rocks in review | Includes glossary and index.
Identifiers: ISBN 9781978537859 (pbk.) | ISBN 9781978537866 (library bound) | ISBN 9781978537873 (ebook)
Subjects: LCSH: Erosion–Juvenile literature.
Classification: LCC QE571.M425 2024 | DDC 551.3'02–dc23

Published in 2024 by
Enslow Publishing
2544 Clinton Street
Buffalo, NY 14224

Copyright © 2024 Enslow Publishing

Portions of this work were originally authored by Frances Nagle and published as *What Is Erosion?* All new material in this edition authored by Anna McDougal.

Designer: Claire Wrazin
Editor: Caitie McAneney

Photo credits: Cover, p. 1 Kelly vanDellen/Shutterstock.com; series art (title & heading background shape) cddesign.co/Shutterstock.com; series art (dark stone background) Somchai kong/Shutterstock.com; series art (white stone header background) Madredus/Shutterstock.com; series art (light stone background) hlinjue/Shutterstock.com; series art (learn more stone background) MaraZe/Shutterstock.com; p. 5 Dudaeva/Shutterstock.com; p. 7 CHC3537/Shutterstock.com; p. 9 Wade Machin/Shutterstock.com; pp. 9, 11 arrows Elina Li/Shutterstock.com; p. 11 Krotnakro/Shutterstock.com; p. 13 Stanley Dullea/Shutterstock.com; p. 15 PapatoniC/Shutterstock.com; p. 17 allstars/Shutterstock.com; pp. 19, 30 Altug Galip/Shutterstock.com; p. 21 VectorMine/Shutterstock.com; p. 22 Alexey Suloev/Shutterstock.com; pp. 23, 30 Valmond/Shutterstock.com; pp. 25, 30 Igor Sh/Shutterstock.com; pp. 27, 30 Salty View/Shutterstock.com; p. 29 nicolabelotti96/Shutterstock.com; p. 30 (mole) kubais/Shutterstock.com.

All rights reserved. No part of this book may be reproduced in any form without permission in writing from the publisher, except by a reviewer.

Printed in the United States of America

CPSIA compliance information: Batch #CWENS24: For further information, contact Enslow Publishing at 1-800-398-2504.

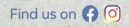

Erosion Rocks!	4
Weathering	6
Moving On	12
Falling	14
Water Works	16
Gone with the Wind	18
A Natural Cycle	20
Amazing Landforms	22
The Downsides of Erosion	26
Shaping Our World	28
How Erosion Happens	30
Glossary	31
For More Information	32
Index	32

Words in the glossary appear in **bold** the first time they are used in the text.

EROSION ROCKS!

Think of a rock you've seen. Maybe it's a small pebble or huge **boulder**. Rocks may seem like they don't change at all. However, rocks often break down and move from place to place. This is called weathering and erosion.

LEARN MORE

Water, wind, and land movement all can move rocks. The pebbles you see on the beach were moved by water.

WEATHERING

Weathering is when rocks break down into bits. The bits are called sediment. **Physical** weathering changes the size and shape of a rock. It happens in different ways. For example, water may flow into a rock and freeze. Then, it cracks the rock.

LEARN MORE

Wind also causes weathering. Wind blows matter at a rock and this chips pieces away.

Sometimes matter such as water and gases change rocks. This matter might break down rocks or change the makeup of their **minerals**. This is called **chemical** weathering. One example is when iron-rich rocks start to rust from **oxygen** in the air.

LEARN MORE

One common chemical weathering example is when rainwater flows into and over rocks. It may carry some matter that breaks down or changes the rock's minerals.

Biological weathering happens when living things weaken and break down rocks. For example, trees may grow through a small crack in a rock, making it bigger. Some animals dig in soil, moving bits of rock to the surface where they may change or move.

LEARN MORE

Lichen is a mix of **algae** and **fungi** that causes holes in rocks. The fungi let out chemicals that break down rock minerals, which are eaten by the algae.

MOVING ON

What happens after weathering? The sediment can either stay in its place or move. Often, the sediment moves and is dropped in a new place. This **process** of movement is erosion. This can happen soon after weathering or a long time after.

LEARN MORE

During sandstorms, which cause erosion, wind moves great amounts of sand from one place to another all at once.

FALLING

Gravity also moves rocks and sediment. Gravity is the force that pulls things down toward Earth's center. If you've ever seen a rock roll downhill, you have seen gravity work as an **agent** of erosion!

LEARN MORE

Sometimes many rocks fall at once. This is called a rockslide.

WATER WORKS

Water is a great agent of erosion. In fact, it causes weathering *and* erosion. As water moves, it wears away at banks and shores. Then, the water carries away the sediment. Rain can also carry soil and sediment as it flows downhill.

LEARN MORE

Beaches often have sand, small rocks, shells, and sediment. The body of water next to the beach **deposits** these things.

GONE WITH THE WIND

Like water, wind can cause both weathering and erosion. It can move sand and rock bits from place to place. As wind moves sediment, that sediment shapes other rocks. It can even wear away at mountains and landforms over time.

LEARN MORE

Sand dunes are landforms that are formed by wind erosion. Some grow thousands of feet tall over time.

A NATURAL CYCLE

Three types of rocks can be found on Earth: igneous, metamorphic, and sedimentary. Through the rock **cycle**, these rocks can change into another kind of rock. One important step in the rock cycle is erosion!

ROCK CYCLE

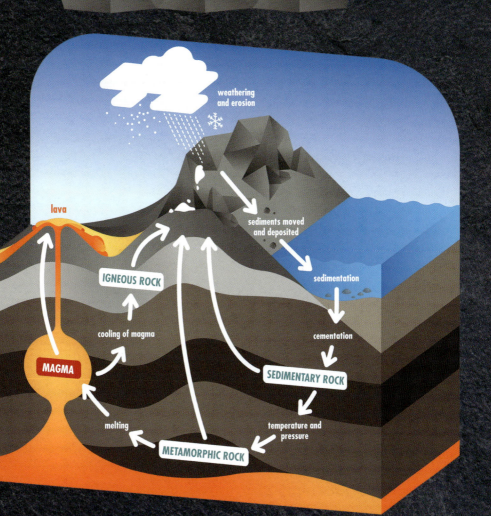

LEARN MORE

The rock cycle is a scientific model that explains how rocks change or break down and become new rocks.

Amazing Landforms

Erosion has created many of the world's greatest landforms. Natural arches, caves, and fjords are just a few examples. Millions of years ago, the Colorado River eroded the rocky land it passed through. It created the Grand Canyon!

Grand Canyon

LEARN MORE

Fjords are long, deep bodies of water with high walls of rock on either side. They were formed by glaciers, or huge masses of ice that move slowly over land.

Waterfalls are also created by erosion. Water flows over layers of hard and soft rock. The softer rock breaks down and erodes more quickly than the harder rock. The rock erodes at different speeds, making the water's path steeper.

LEARN MORE

One of the most famous waterfalls in the world is Niagara Falls. Rushing waters between Lake Erie and Lake Ontario eroded land, creating a river that passes over a steep cliff.

Niagara Falls

THE DOWNSIDES OF EROSION

Erosion may cause damage, or harm, and even cost lives. Mudslides and rockslides can block roads and bury homes. Wind can carry soil away from farms, harming crops. When land erodes, it may ruin the **habitats** of native plants and animals.

LEARN MORE

People can plant more trees and plants to reduce soil erosion. People can also direct extra rainwater from storms to safer places.

SHAPING OUR WORLD

Erosion is a key natural process that has shaped our world. Some erosion processes take millions of years, while others work quickly. The next time you see a landform, think about how erosion may have played a part in its story!

LEARN MORE

It took some glaciers more than a million years to carve out valleys!

WIND

WATER

HOW EROSION HAPPENS

GLACIERS

GRAVITY

PEOPLE and ANIMALS

GLOSSARY

agent: Something that produces an effect.

algae: Plantlike living things that are mostly found in water.

boulder: A very large rock.

chemical: Having to do with matter that can be mixed with other matter to cause changes. Also, the matter itself.

cycle: A sequence of events that repeats.

deposit: To let fall or sink.

fungus: A living thing that is somewhat like a plant, but doesn't make its own food, have leaves, or have a green color. The plural form is fungi.

habitat: The natural place where an animal or plant lives.

mineral: Matter in the ground that forms rocks.

oxygen: A colorless, odorless gas that many animals, including people, need to breathe.

physical: Having to do with a form that can be seen or touched.

process: A natural continuing action.

FOR MORE INFORMATION

BOOKS

Orr, Tamra. *Erosion.* North Mankato, MN: Pebble Books, 2021.

Rogers, Marie. *Exploring Weathering and Erosion.* New York, NY: PowerKids Press, 2022.

WEBSITE

Erosion
www.ducksters.com/science/earth_science/erosion.php
Explore more fun facts about erosion and its effects.

Publisher's note to educators and parents: Our editors have carefully reviewed this website to ensure it is suitable for students. Many websites change frequently, however, and we cannot guarantee that a site's future contents will continue to meet our high standards of quality and educational value. Be advised that students should be closely supervised whenever they access the internet.

INDEX

animals, 10, 26, 30
fjords, 22, 23
glacier, 23, 29, 30
Grand Canyon, 22
gravity, 14, 30
lichen, 10
rockslide, 14, 26

rust, 8
sand dunes, 19
sediment, 6, 12, 14, 16, 17, 18
soil, 10, 16, 26, 27
trees, 10, 27
waterfalls, 24